THE
Alfred d'Auberge
PIANO
COURSE

BOOK FIVE

ALFRED PUBLISHING CO., INC.

designed and illustrated by ERNIE BARTH

contents

MERRY WIDOW WALTZ 3

I AM THE VERY MODEL OF A MODERN MAJOR GENERAL 4

YANKEE DOODLE DANDY 6

AMERICA, THE BEAUTIFUL 8

TECHNIC-TONE-TOUCH 9

SKATERS WALTZ 10

MORE ABOUT INTERVALS 12

OUR BOYS 13
    Interval Quiz

DANCING DOLL 14

THE GOLDEN WEDDING 16
    Four New Musical Signs

HUNGARIAN DANCE No. 5 17

SHEPHERD'S HEY 18
    With Five L. H. Accompaniments

THOUSAND AND ONE NIGHTS 19
    Introducing the Long Crescendo

TO A WILD ROSE 20

DOTTED EIGHTH NOTES 22
    County Fair

BATTLE HYMN OF THE REPUBLIC 23

COUNTRY GARDENS 24

THE BEGINNING OF COUNTERPOINT 26

HYMN OF THANKSGIVING 27

RONDO 28
    Note Review

COMIN' THRO' THE RYE 30
    Introducing the Scotch Snap

RUSTIC DANCE 31

TURKISH MARCH (Beethoven) 32

MELODY IN F 34

THE TURN 35

MINUET (Paderewski) 36

TURKISH MARCH (Mozart) 38

THE CUCKOO 40
    Study in Reading Three Staves

PARADE OF THE TIN SOLDIERS 41

LA CUCARACHA 44

CLAIR DE LUNE 45

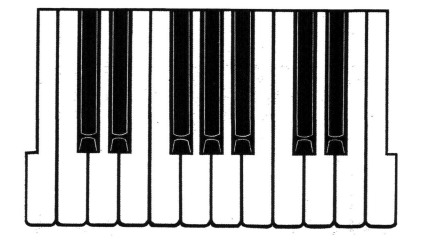

FRANZ LEHAR, composer of the world-sweeping operetta "The Merry Widow," was born in Komorn, Hungary, April 30, 1870. He was educated at the Prague Conservatory and at 18, made his debut as a violinist. He conducted the Tonkünstlers Orchestra in Vienna where his Merry Widow was first produced in 1905. He composed many brilliant operettas although his first two were failures.

Merry Widow Waltz

LEHAR

The comic opera "THE PIRATES OF PENZANCE" is a topsy-turvy world of tender-hearted pirates who are not pirates at all, but noblemen; and of Frederic, who was to be apprenticed to a pilot, but through the deafness of his guardian, was apprenticed to a pirate. There is the Major General and his large family of daughters whom the pirates capture. Frederic organizes a police expedition to seize the pirates; the police are defeated, but the sergeant calls on the victorious pirates to yield in the Queen's name, a claim on their loyalty which they cannot resist.

I am the very model of a
MODERN MAJOR GENERAL

from "The Pirates of Penzance" by GILBERT and SULLIVAN

I am the ver-y mod-el of a mod-ern Ma-jor Gen-er-al: I've

in-for-ma-tion veg-e-ta-ble, an-i-mal, and min-er-al; I

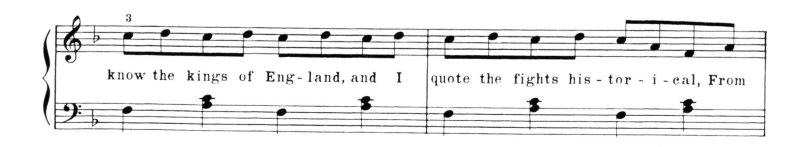

know the kings of Eng-land, and I quote the fights his-tor-i-cal, From

Mar - a - thon to Wa - ter - loo, in or - der cat - e - gor - i - cal; I'm

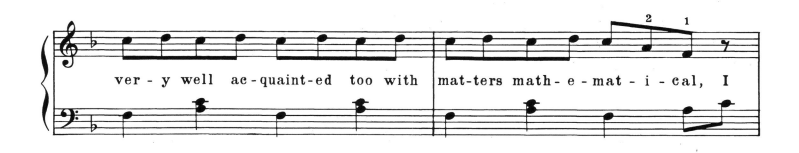

ver - y well ac - quaint - ed too with mat - ters math - e - mat - i - cal, I

un - der - stand e - qua - tions both the sim - ple and quad - rat - i - cal, In

short, in mat - ters veg - e - ta - ble, an - i - mal, and min - er - al, I

am the ver - y mod - el of a mod - ern Ma - jor Gen - er - al!

GEORGE M. COHAN, born in Providence, R. I., July 4, 1878 was an actor, dramatist, producer, and song writer. He made his first stage appearance at the age of 9, and wrote many plays in which he also acted. Of his many songs, "Over There" is recognized as the best song of World War I. Other famous songs are ":Mary is a Grand Old Name," "You're a Grand Old Flag," "Give My Regards to Broadway," and "Yankee Doodle Dandy." He was intensely patriotic, very proud of being born on the 4th of July, and liked to call himself a nephew of Uncle Sam.

YANKEE DOODLE DANDY

COHAN

Allegro

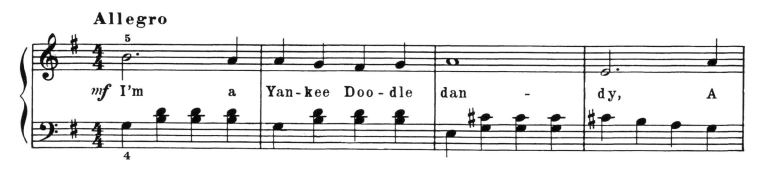

I'm   a   Yan-kee Doo-dle   dan   -   dy,   A

Yan   -   kee   Doo - dle,   do   or   die;   A

real   live   neph - ew   of   my   Un - cle   Sam's,

Born on the Fourth of Ju - ly. I've

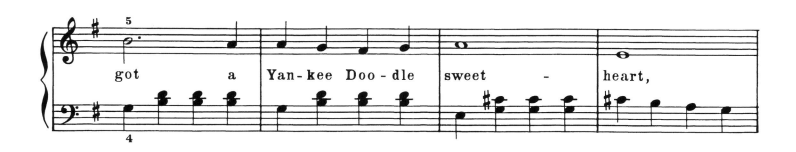

got a Yan-kee Doo - dle sweet - heart,

She's my Yan - kee Doo - dle joy.

f Yan-kee Doo-dle came to Lon-don, Just to ride the po - nies,

I am a Yan - kee Doo - dle boy.

AMERICA,
the beautiful

WARD-BATES

This is one of the most popular of American patriotic songs. The words were written in 1893 by KATHERINE LEE BATES, an American poet and educator, on her return from a trip to the summit of Pike's Peak. They were published in 1895 and have been sung to numerous tunes. This version, set to the music of "Materna" by Samuel A. Ward, is the most famous.

O beau-ti-ful for spa-cious skies, For am-ber waves of grain, For pur-ple moun-tain ma-jes-ties a-bove the fruit-ed plain. A-mer-i-ca! A-mer-i-ca! God shed His grace on thee, And crown thy good with bro-ther-hood from sea to shin-ing sea.

TECHNIC · TONE · TOUCH

 Brilliant playing depends more on clarity than speed. Begin these exercises in the tempo which you can play each note clean and clearly. When the slower tempo is perfect, increase the speed on each repetition.

You can also develop independence of the hands and control of tone by practising the exercises in these 3 styles:

FOR INDEPENDENCE OF THE HANDS: Ex. #1; R. H. legato, L. H. staccato. Ex. #2; L. H. legato, R. H. staccato:
FOR TONE CONTROL: one measure *f*, one measure *p*.
FOR TONE SHADINGS: one measure crescendo, one measure diminuendo.

EMIL WALDTEUFEL, composer of nearly 250 dance pieces and immensely successful waltzes, was born in Strasbourg, Alsace, Dec. 9, 1837. He was educated in the Paris Conservatoire, was appointed court pianist and composer to Empress Eugenie, and conducted the court balls and entertainments for Napoleon III. He died Feb. 16, 1915 in Paris, after a very successful career, and great rivalry between himself and Johann (the Waltz King) Strauss.

SKATERS WALTZ

WALDTEUFEL

more about INTERVALS

We have learned that an INTERVAL is the distance from one note to another. They are figured upwards from the lowest note, in steps, like the alphabet.

For example: C to E is 3 steps; 1   2   3 . . . therefore, C to E is the INTERVAL of a 3rd.

C to A is 6 steps, 1   2   3   4   5   6 . . . therefore, C to A is the INTERVAL of a 6th.

The 3rds and 6ths are called CONSONANT INTERVALS, that is, agreeable, restful. The following are all 3rds, therefore they are all CONSONANT INTERVALS. . . . .

The intervals 2nds, 4ths, 5ths, and 7ths are called DISSONANT INTERVALS, that is, inharmonious. The following are all DISSONANT INTERVALS: . . . .

Accidentals do not effect the "number" of the INTERVAL. The following are all 3rds: . . . . . .

In the square below each INTERVAL, write the name of the INTERVAL: 2nd, 3rd, 4th, 5th, 6th, or 7th.

In the square below each INTERVAL, mark whether it is Consonant or Dissonant.

In the squares below each INTERVAL, mark the "number" of the INTERVAL and whether it is Consonant or Dissonant.

INTERVAL QUIZ

The right hand of this song has all the intervals learned on the preceding page. After you have learned to play this piece, mark above each interval whether it is a 2nd, 3rd, 4th, 5th, 6th, or 7th.

Our BOYS

Allegro

The BOOGIE-WOOGIE effect in the LEFT HAND may be played as though written:

EDUARD POLDINI was born in Budapest, June 13, 1869. He composed operas, a ballet, and several children's operas. His "Vagabond Princess" was performed in 1903 in Budapest; two operas were produced in London, and "Wedding Carnival" was the most popular opera of the State Opera House in Budapest. He is famous for his many piano pieces, including the very popular "Dancing Doll."

dancing DOLL

POLDINI

 **introducing**

FOUR
NEW MUSICAL
SIGNS

① ⌢ slightly staccato.

② ♫ ♪ two grace notes preceding the beat (unaccented appoggiature).

③ *sfz* sforzando, struck with emphasis (louder than an accent).

④ *tr* ♪ the trill ending on the lower note.

the GOLDEN WEDDING

Moderato

GABRIEL-MARIE

As a young man, JOHANNES BRAHMS was a brilliant pianist and made many concert tours with the great Hungarian violinist Remenyi. Through this association, Brahms absorbed the beauty of Hungarian folk music which resulted in his many very popular arrangements of Hungarian dances. This music was influenced by the Magyars, who are closer related to the Turks than their neighbors the Poles and Russians. The profusion of ornamentation characterizing much Hungarian music was imported from the Orient by the Gypsies, who, although they are the national musicians of Hungary, are basically a Hindu people.

HUNGARIAN DANCE No. 5

BRAHMS

* *8va ad lib.* = PLAY AN OCTAVE HIGHER IF YOU WISH.

SHEPHERD'S HEY

with FIVE DIFFERENT L. H. ACCOMPANIMENTS

Each line may be considered an individual exercise, and should be repeated many times if it presents any particular difficulty.

Thousand and One Nights

☀ introducing the LONG CRESCENDO

EDWARD A. MacDOWELL, America's greatest tone-master and most eminent composer, was born in New York, Dec. 18, 1861. His principal piano teacher was Teresa Carreno, who helped publicize his works and to whom he dedicated his 2nd Piano Concerto. His first piano suite was performed through the influence of Liszt. In 1888 he settled in Boston, teaching and concertizing. In 1896 he became the first head of the new department of music at Columbia University. Of his three remarkable piano sonatas, the 3rd, dedicated to Grieg, was described as "an epic of rainbow and thunder."

to a WILD ROSE

MacDOWELL

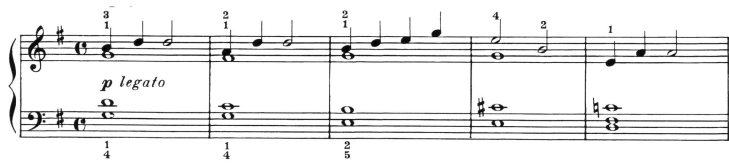

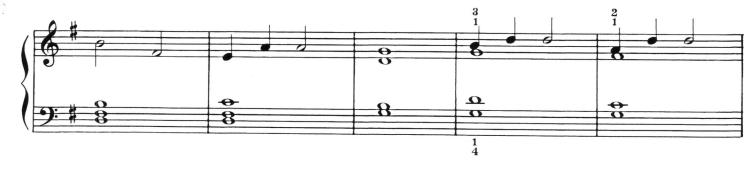

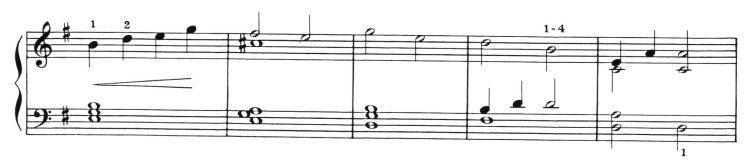

DOTTED EIGHTH NOTES

A DOTTED EIGHTH NOTE has the same value as an eighth note tied to a sixteenth note.

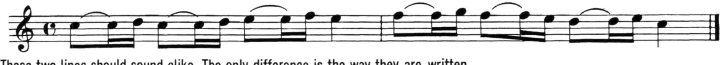

These two lines should sound alike. The only difference is the way they are written.

COUNTY FAIR

Moderato

Battle Hymn of the Republic

JULIA WARD HOWE, who wrote the poem to this stirring war song was born in New York, May 27, 1819. In December of 1861, she and her husband, Dr. S. G. Howe, visited Washington. The city was full of soldiers and everywhere the "watchfires of a hundred circling camps" could be seen. They traveled through the war-torn area, escorted by Federal soldiers who sang the popular Civil War songs, including "John Brown's Body." Inspired by its stirring rhythm, Julia Howe wrote new verses to the music, calling it the "Battle Hymn of the Republic."

STEFFE-HOWE

MORRIS DANCE

The MORRIS DANCE was an English country-dance which derived its name from the Moors among whom it originated. It was probably brought to England in the time of Edward III, (1312-1377) when John of Gaunt returned from Spain. The dancers wore ankle-bells and grotesque costumes. The tunes of various kinds were played on a Pipe.

TABOR

PIPE

The rhythm was played on a TABOR. It was hung around the neck and beaten with a stick held in the right hand while the left hand was fingering the Pipe.

COUNTRY GARDENS

Allegro

MORRIS DANCE

the beginning of COUNTERPOINT

In the 7th century, the Christian Church, attempting to establish a system for learning the many chants, experimented with its first musical notation. This music writing consisted of a series of hooks and curves, called NEUMES from the Greek word meaning signs.

These NEUMES 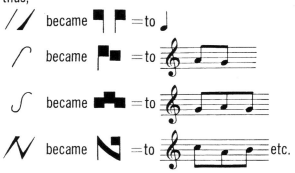 did not give the pitch, but were merely reminders when the music (in a chant already learned) ascended or descended. Later, the neumes developed into the square notes called punctus or punctum, thus;

When a second voice, at a different pitch was added, they called it PUNCTUS CONTRA PUNCTUM (note against note) from which the word COUNTERPOINT was derived.

Counterpoint is therefore simply two melodies that harmonize when played together. If you play Humoresque with one hand, and Swanee River with the other, you have counterpoint.

HUMORESQUE

SWANEE RIVER

In COUNTERPOINT, the principal melody is called the FIXED MELODY.

If the SECOND MELODY may be played **above** the FIXED MELODY and still harmonizes,

. . . it is called DOUBLE, or INVERTED COUNTERPOINT.

hymn of THANKSGIVING

Andante

We gath - er to - geth - er to ask the Lord's bless - ing, He chast - ens and hast - ens His will to make known; The wick - ed op - press - ing cease them from dis - tress - ing, Sing prais - es to His name, He for - gets not His own.

MUZIO CLEMENTI was born 1752 in Rome. A prolific composer and teacher whose many eminent pupils include Field, Moscheles and Meyerbeer. He made his debut as a pianist in London, and at 18, composed his famous Op. 11 (the basis of the modern piano sonata) of which K. P. Bach said, "Only the devil and Clementi could play it." In 1780, in Paris, he was given a remarkable reception and called the greatest player of the age with the possible exception of Mozart whom he once met in a "friendly" competition. His compositions include 106 piano sonatas, chamber works, many books of studies and the standard book of etudes, "Gradus ad Parnassum."

RONDO
(NOTE REVIEW)

comin' thro' the RYE

Moderato

SCOTCH AIR

When a DOTTED 8th and 16th is written ♪. instead of the usual ♪. it is called the **SCOTCH SNAP**.

RUSTIC DANCE

LUDWIG VAN BEETHOVEN was born in Bonn-on-Rhine, Dec. 16, 1770. From his 4th year, his father taught him music; at 8 he was a good violinist, and at 11 played Bach's Well-Tempered Clavichord. He took some lessons from Mozart, then went to Vienna to study counterpoint with Haydn. He played his C Major Piano Concerto at his first public concert in 1795; the following year he played for King Wilhelm II, and in 1798 had sensational concerts in Prague. Before he was thirty, he was considered the greatest of all clavier composers. In other music, only Mozart and Haydn were regarded as his equals. His great "Eroica" symphony was dedicated to Napoleon Bonaparte for advocating liberty, equality, and fraternity, but when Napoleon proclaimed himself Emperor, Beethoven, in a rage, tore up the title-page and dedication.

Turkish March

Allegro

from "The Ruins of Athens" by BEETHOVEN

ANTON RUBINSTEIN was born Nov. 30, 1830 in Bessarabia, Russia. One of the world's greatest pianists, his first teacher was his mother, then when 7, he was taken to Moscow where his father had a pencil factory. At 9, he made a concert tour, and at 10, played for Chopin and Liszt. He founded the Imperial Conservatory at St. Petersburg, toured Europe with the greatest success and gave 215 concerts in America. As a pianist he was second only to Liszt, and of his remarkable singing touch, a critic wrote, "He was the only man who could play the violin on the piano." He composed a great amount of music, including "Sacred Opera," the form he created.

melody in F

RUBINSTEIN

the TURN

The Turn is an embellishment, like the trills, grace notes, etc. The sign ∞ is a development of the notation of the 9th and 10th centuries, when music writing consisted of dots and lines, and signs and symbols of many shapes:

9th Century

10th Century

Later, other signs were invented to indicate the melody:

A half circle (circumflex sign) ⌒

meant

The reversed circumflex ⌣

meant

Short, thick strokes

meant

thick and thin strokes

meant

Two circumflex signs were joined

indicating

the
origin
of
our modern sign,

the TURN...

Placed over any note (called the PRINCIPAL NOTE) means to play ....

THE PRINCIPAL NOTE

THE NOTE ABOVE

THE PRINCIPAL NOTE

THE NOTE A HALF STEP BELOW

FINISH ON THE PRINCIPAL NOTE.

This creates a group of 5 equal notes played in one beat. The five notes are called a Quintuplet, and marked

⌒5 or 5

WRITTEN   PLAYED

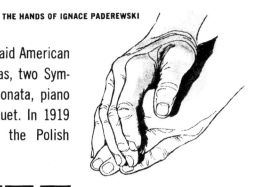

IGNACE PADEREWSKI, a phenominally success-ful pianist, was born in Podolia, Poland, Nov. 6, 1860. He was educated in Vienna, Berlin, and the Warsaw Conservatory where he later taught piano. His success as a pianist was unpre-cedented in Europe and America. In 1896 he established the Paderewski fund to aid American composers. He composed two operas, two Sym-phonies, a Piano concerto, Violin Sonata, piano pieces, songs, and the popular Minuet. In 1919 he became the first Premier of the Polish Republic.

MINUET

PADEREWSKI

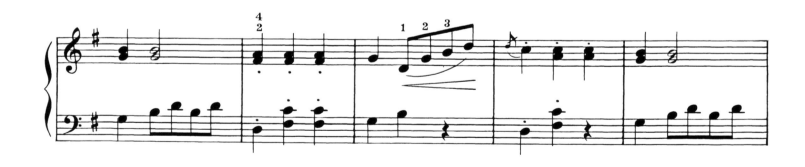

WOLFGANG AMADEUS MOZART was born in Salzburg, Jan. 27, 1756. Probably the greatest musical genius of all time, he began composing when he was 5, and at 6, made a joint debut with his sister in Munich. When 7, he appeared in Paris where his sonatas were published. The following year, he was in London, playing for royalty and astounding the audiences with his remarkable playing, sight-reading and improvising. When 11, he composed an Oratorio, and the opera "La Finta Semplice." Conducted his own Mass when he was 12, and at 14 played his own symphony. In 1787, after a successful production of his "Don Giovanni" in Prague, the Emperor appointed him chamber composer. In 1791, he contracted typhus and died Dec. 5. In his 35 years, he created more masterpieces than any great composer before him, or since. His more than 600 works include 41 symphonies; 43 violin sonatas; 25 piano concertos; 6 violin concertos; 7 string quartets; 15 Masses; arias; songs; and some of his era's purest church music. He died destitute, and amidst a violent rain-storm, was placed in a common grave in a potter's field, never since discovered.

Turkish March

MOZART

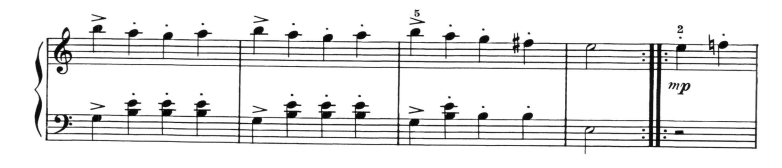

the CUCKOO

a study in READING THREE STAVES

CLAUDE L. DAQUIN was a celebrated organist and composer, born 1694 in Paris, died 1772. In this famous arrangement, the high C and A, sounding the call of the cuckoo, must be played slightly louder than the other notes.

DAQUIN

PARADE of the TIN SOLDIERS

Allegretto

LEON JESSEL

La Cucaracha RUMBA

The RUMBA is a Cuban dance of African origin. It has heavily accented rhythms and complicated syncopation. The dance is primarily movements of the body rather than the feet.

Allegro Moderato

CLAUDE DEBUSSY was born in Paris, August 22, 1862. The poet of French music and the founder of impressionism, he was a pupil at the Paris Conservatoire and won the Grand Prix de Rome with his Cantata "L'Enfant Prodigue." His "Pelleas et Melisande" based on Maeterlinck's play was a sensation at the Opera Comique in Paris. He composed many important orchestral works, Operas, Sonatas, songs and many piano works.

Clair De Lune from SUITE BERGAMASQUE

Moderato espressivo

DEBUSSY

* MOLTO — much, very.

certificate of promotion

THIS CERTIFIES THAT _____

HAS MASTERED AND PERFECTED

BOOK 5 OF THE ALFRED d'AUBERGE PIANO COURSE

AND IS HEREBY PROMOTED INTO

BOOK 6 OF THE ALFRED d'AUBERGE PIANO COURSE

_____ TEACHER

_____ DATE